Librarians

Community Workers

by Alice K. Flanagan

Content Adviser: Judy King,
American Library Association

Reading Adviser: Dr. Linda D. Labbo,
College of Education, Department of Reading Education,
The University of Georgia

 COMPASS POINT BOOKS

Minneapolis, Minnesota

Compass Point Books
3722 West 50th Street, #115
Minneapolis, MN 55410

Visit Compass Point Books on the Internet at *www.compasspointbooks.com* or e-mail your
request to *custserv@compasspointbooks.com*

Photographs ©:
Gregg Andersen, cover; Sally VanderLaan/Visuals Unlimited, 4, 17, 20; Photri-Microstock/Jeff Greenberg, 5; Unicorn
Stock Photos/Jeff Greenberg, 6; James L. Shaffer, 7, 9, 15, 19, 22, 24, 26; Jeff Greenberg/Visuals
Unlimited, 8, 18, 27; Unicorn Stock Photos/Remi, 10; Jim Pickerell/FPG International, 11; Pictor, 12, 13, 23;
Unicorn Stock Photos/Martha McBride, 14; Pictor/Bob Daemmrich, 16; Eric Anderson/Visuals Unlimited, 21;
Cheryl Ertelt/Visuals Unlimited, 25.

Editors: E. Russell Primm and Emily J. Dolbear
Photo Researcher: Svetlana Zhurkina
Photo Selector: Linda S. Koutris
Designer: Bradfordesign, Inc.

Library of Congress Cataloging-in-Publication Data

Flanagan, Alice K.
     Librarians / by Alice K. Flanagan.
       p. cm. — (Community workers)
     Includes bibliographical references and index.
     ISBN 0-7565-0063-X (lib. bdg.)
     1. Librarians—Juvenile literature. 2. Library science—Vocational guidance—Juvenile literature.
3. Libraries—Juvenile literature. [1. Librarians. 2. Libraries. 3. Occupations.] I. Title. II. Series.
     Z682 .F58 2001
     020'.92—dc21   00-011717

Table of Contents

What Do Librarians Do?

Librarians run libraries. They help people find books, magazines, newspapers, and tapes. They also help people find specific information. Librarians often organize programs, such as story hours for children and lectures for adults. After all, libraries are for everyone.

Librarians make sure that books are shelved properly.

A school librarian works with students.

Where Do They Work?

Many librarians work in **public libraries**. Others work in school or university libraries. Some librarians manage special libraries in hospitals or businesses. Sometimes librarians work in a **bookmobile**. They bring books, audiotapes, and videotapes to people who cannot come to the library.

This librarian works in a public library.

Many schools have their own libraries.

Who Do They Work With?

Librarians work mostly with the public. They get help from librarians at other libraries. They also get help from library workers who check out books and clean the building. Librarians also work with people who sell books and computer systems.

◀ These librarians review books together.

A librarian shows young people how to use the library. ▶

School librarians help teachers with their classes. They work with students on special projects. School librarians read stories to children. They also help young people find fun books to read.

◄ A children's story hour in the classroom

Children enjoy ▶ visits to the school library.

What Training Does It Take?

All librarians have a college degree. Many librarians earn a higher degree in **library science**. This degree helps them manage a library. School librarians also need a degree in teaching.

A library professor teaches class in the library.

Librarians who want to work in a school must earn a teaching degree.

What Tools and Equipment Do They Use?

Librarians use many kinds of machines. They use a **scanner** to check out books. They use computers to search the Internet and the **library catalog**. In the past, this listing was kept on index cards. Librarians also use **audiovisual equipment**, such as slide projectors and **microfilm readers**.

A librarian uses a scanner to check out a book.

A librarian checks information on the Internet.

What Skills Do Librarians Need?

Librarians need planning and people skills. They manage the library's workers. They manage the library's money too. Today's librarians also need good computer skills.

A librarian works with a young student to find information.

Librarians need to be able to use computers.

Librarians need to understand what people in the library are looking for. So they have to be good listeners. They need to have good memories too. Librarians also have to be organized.

Librarians sometimes use videotapes to help people learn about the library.

A librarian must be organized.

What Problems Do They Face?

Working with the public can be trying. Sometimes, people do not take care of the library's things. Librarians must work to keep the library in good order. And they have limited money to buy what the library needs. But a librarian's biggest problem may be finding time to read!

◀ Librarians make sure that books are easy to find.

Some people don't take care of their library books. ▶

How Do They Help?

Librarians encourage reading and learning. They protect information about history and **literature**. They help people in business and universities. Without libraries, there would be no free place to get books to learn about our world.

A librarian shares new items with young readers.

A librarian uses computer software to help a child learn to read.

Would You Like to Be a Librarian?

Do you love to read? Do you like books and computers? Maybe you would like to be a librarian someday. You can prepare now. At home, read to a brother or sister. Visit the library often. Ask librarians if you can help them. In school, learn how to find information in books and on the computer. Help others find information too.

◄ If you like to read, you might enjoy working as a librarian.

The love of books begins early! ▶

A Librarian's Tools

security gate

computer terminal

scanner

computer keyboard

reference book

In the Library

bookshelves

patron

librarian

study table

reference desk

reference books

A Librarian's Day

Morning
- A librarian arrives at the library. She turns on all the computers and prepares for the day's visitors.
- The librarian reads to children as part of the preschool learning program.
- After the reading program, the librarian helps put returned books back on the shelves.
- She helps a visitor find a best-selling book.

Noon
- The librarian takes a short break for lunch. She reads the newspaper to keep up on current events.

Afternoon
- The librarian helps students find books for school reports.
- She checks out books and collects fines for overdue books.
- She answers students' questions about looking for information on the Internet.

Evening
- After everyone has left, she turns off all the computers and other equipment. Then the librarian closes the library.
- She attends a dinner for a local group that teaches adults to read.
- At home, she reads reviews of new books she may want to buy for the library.

Glossary

audiovisual equipment—machines that use sound and pictures to teach things

bookmobile—a van or bus used as a small traveling library

library catalog—a listing of all the library's books and tapes

library science—the study of library care and management

literature—written works such as novels, plays, short stories, and poems

microfilm readers—machines that allow people to read printed pages stored on filmstrips

public libraries—places that provide books and other materials free to everyone

scanner—a machine that records information

Did You Know?

- Most libraries have only one professional librarian.

- The United States has more than 122,000 libraries of all kinds.

- More than 127,000 professional librarians work in public, academic, and school libraries in the United States.

- The Library of Congress in Washington, D.C., is the largest library in the world. It has almost 119 million items. It also has 530 miles (853 kilometers) of bookshelves.

Want to Know More?

At the Library

Flanagan, Alice K., and Christine Osinski (photographer). *Ms. Davison, Our Librarian*. Danbury, Conn.: Children's Press, 1997.

Kottke, Jan. *A Day with a Librarian*. Danbury, Conn.: Children's Press, 2000.

Reedy, Dee. *Librarians*. Mankato, Minn.: Bridgestone Books, 1998.

On the Web

Kids Connect: Ask KC

http://www.ala.org/ICONN/AskKC.html

For the chance to ask librarians questions

The Library of Congress

http://www.loc.gov

For information from the largest library in the world

Through the Mail

American Library Association

Public Information Office

50 E. Huron Street

Chicago, IL 60611

To get information about libraries and librarians

On the Road

The Library of Congress

101 Independence Avenue, S.W.

Washington, DC 20540

202/707-5000

To see the largest U.S. library collection as well as great exhibits

Index

About the Author

Alice K. Flanagan writes books for children and teachers. Since she was a young girl, she has enjoyed writing. She has written more than seventy books on a wide variety of topics. Some of her books include biographies of U.S. presidents and their wives, biographies of people working in our neighborhoods, phonics books for beginning readers, and informational books about birds and Native Americans. Alice K. Flanagan lives in Chicago, Illinois.